HOW TO C

MW00947680

LEFT-HANDED

CROCHET PATTERNS FOR LEFT-HANDED GUIDE

Copyright © 2023

DEDICATION

Contents

HOW TO CROCHET LEFT-HANDED

ULTIMATE GUIDE TO LEFT-HANDED CROCHET

Many of the left-handed crafters who learned to crochet decades ago had to learn the craft "backwards" from their natural approach because they learned from a right-handed crocheter. Today, that's no longer necessary. There are teachers, tutorials, patterns and more for the left-handed crocheter.

In this guide, you'll learn the basic stitches in left-handed crochet, tips for learning more, information on finding left-handed pattern sources and guidance for adapting existing patterns to your left-handed crochet style. Are you a right-handed crocheter who wants to teach a leftie how to crochet? There's information on that in this guide, too!

BASIC UNDERSTANDING OF LEFT-HANDED CROCHET

Left-handed crochet is basically a mirror-image of right-handed crochet. The left-handed crocheter holds the crochet hook in his or her left hand and the yarn in the right hand. Learning how to hold the hook (in either "pencil grip" or "knife grip") and manipulate the yarn is similar to learning as a right-handed crafter; follow your teachers and tutorials but also figure out what works best for you.

The majority of crochet tutorials, and nearly all crochet patterns and symbol charts, are written for right-handed crochet. In left-handed crochet, you follow the exact same instructions, but you work in the opposite direction.

HOW TO CROCHET LEFT-HANDED

This means that when you are working rows, row one will be worked into the foundation chain starting on the left side and working towards the right. This should feel fairly natural to you as a left-hander. It also means that when youareworking in rounds, you will be crocheting clockwise, rather than the counter-clockwise way that righties are working.

HOW TO CROCHET CHAIN LEFT-HANDED

STEP 1

Begin with a slip knot.

HOW TO CROCHET LEFT-HANDED

STEP 2

Yarn over. Note that every time you "yarn over" in your crochet work, you will be scooping the yarn clockwise with your hook to pick up the yarn.

HOW TO CROCHET LEFT-HANDED

STEP 3

Draw hook through loop. You'll scoop the yarn clockwise here.

STEP 4

Repeat steps 2-3; each repetition is one chain.

HOW TO SINGLE CROCHET LEFT-HANDED

STEP 1

Crochet a foundation chain of any length.

HOW TO CROCHET LEFT-HANDED

STEP 2

Insert hook into second chain from hook. Your hook will be held in your left hand, the chain will be extending out to the right, and you will insert the hook into the second chainthat is to the right of the hook.

HOW TO CROCHET LEFT-HANDED

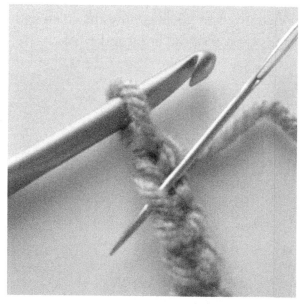

HOW TO CROCHET LEFT-HANDED

This photo demonstrates how you'll go into the chain with your hook, so you have 2 stands on top of the hook and 1 below.

STEP 3

Yarn over.

STEP 4

Draw through loop. You will see two loops on your hook at the end of this step.

HOW TO CROCHET LEFT-HANDED

STEP 5

Yarn over.

STEP 6

Draw through both loops on hook. This is your first sc.

STEP 7

Insert hook into next chain and repeat steps 3-6.

STEP 8

Repeat step 7 across row.

HOW TO DOUBLE CROCHET LEFT-HANDED

HOW TO CROCHET LEFT-HANDED

STEP 1

Crochet a foundation chain of any length.

STEP 2

Yarn over.

HOW TO CROCHET LEFT-HANDED

STEP 3

Insert hook into fourth chain from hook. This is the fourth chain towards the right, working from left to right away from your hook.

HOW TO CROCHET LEFT-HANDED

STEP 4

Yarn over.

HOW TO CROCHET LEFT-HANDED

STEP 5

Draw through loop. You will see three loops on your hook at the end
of this step.

STEP 6

Yarn over and draw through the first two of those three loops on the hook.

STEP 7

Yarn over and draw through the two loops now on the hook. You've completed your first double crochet.

HOW TO CROCHET LEFT-HANDED

HOW TO CROCHET LEFT-HANDED

STEP 8

Yarn over and insert crochet hook into the next stitch then repeat steps 4-7 for the next stitch.

STEP 9

Repeat step 8 across row.

STEP 10

Turn work. Chain 3 for turning chain.

STEP 11

Yarn over and insert hook into next stitch.

HOW TO CROCHET LEFT-HANDED

In the photo above, Rachel shows that you are crocheting your next stitch into the 3rd chain of the turning chain from the previous row. She explains, "this ensures stitch count remains correct and shape is not triangular; I made plenty of accidental 'bunting' when I was learning!" Repeat your dc stitches across the entire row.

IMPORTANT TIPS FOR LEFT-HANDED CROCHET

HOW TO CROCHET LEFT-HANDED

This photo depicts the "wrong side" of double crochet stitch, as described below.

- Leave your beginning yarn tail hanging at the start of each project (don't crochet over it); when a pattern mentions the "right side" or "wrong side" of the work, look for that tail as a cue. The "right side" will be when the tail is on the bottom right corner.

- Remember that every time you yarn over, you are going to "scoop the yarn clockwise". Rachel says that she repeated this mantra to herself regularly when first learning to crochet.

- Left-handed crochet is possible to do with both written patterns and visual ones. With charts and graphs, you can reverse the image (see below in the section on adapting existing patterns) and use the reversed image as your guide.

A close up of the crochet jasmine stitch being worked left handed.

The Truth About Left-Handed Crochet: The Differences For Left Handed Crocheters

Over the years I have been crocheting I have seen all sorts of comments on social media and the internet about those who crochet left handed.

From sweeping statements like 'you can't follow patterns if you're left handed ' (this is nonsense) to 'left handed crochet looks different' (this is only true in specific circumstances) and 'it's harder to learn to crochet if you're left handed' (only if you're using right handed resources).

There are a ton of myths and misinterpretations out there about what

HOW TO CROCHET LEFT-HANDED

it means to be a left handed crocheter.

As a left handed crocheter, designer and crochet pattern writer, I want to use my personal experience to address some of these misunderstandings and explain the differences between left and right handed crochet.

I'll explain what the practical differences are for left handed vs right handed crocheters and dig into how these can be managed and mitigated if needed.

I never want to see a left hander put off crochet because someone on a facebook group says they can't do something – because you can!

According to stats, about 1 in 9 of the population are left handed. This proportion seems to have been fairly stable throughout the years. If you're left handed, you'll know that it comes with both challenges and benefits.

Many tools are designed with right handers only in mind, and their left handed counterparts are often much more expensive. Thankfully, this generally isn't the case for crochet hooks, which can be used in either hand.

Today I'm going to share my experiences of what it's like to learn to crochet left handed, and to design and write crochet patterns as a left handed designer.

HOW TO CROCHET LEFT-HANDED

So let's get into how crochet differs for left handed folks

What Is The Difference Between Left And Right Handed Crochet?

Left and right handed crocheters work in opposite directions:

A right handed crocheter will work in rows from right to left and in the round anticlockwise.

A left handed crocheter works a row from left to right and a in the round clockwise.

A left handed crochet project would be a mirror image of the same project made by a right handed crocheter.

For example, a simple swatch of rows of double crochet made by a left handed crocheter will be a flipped version of that made by a right handed crocheter. Though it would take very close examination to notice any differences between the two.

That really is the long and the short of it.

(Note there are always exceptions and crocheters who use their own unique style.)

What do you need to know about being a left handed crocheter?

Generally speaking, a left hander can follow the same patterns as a right hander.

However, visuals created by right handers may need mentally flipping

HOW TO CROCHET LEFT-HANDED

or mirroring in a leftie's head.

As a left-hander, I have gotten used to mentally reversing a lot of the right handed world because it's what's needed to to get along. Although this can feel like a challenge, I like to think that it keeps our brains nimble and flexible. Anytime I have to flip something with my mind, I think of it as a mini brain workout to keep me on my toes.

With crochet, you will find this skill useful when it comes to video or picture tutorials and some charts / crochet diagrams.

I'll go into a bit more detail about these below, but I want to say that if you struggle with reversing images in your mind, don't fret, there is another way…

If mentally working backwards leaves you all fingers and thumbs then you can take a mirror, hold it to the resource you're working from and view it from the image in the mirror rather than the one on the screen.

What should left handed crocheters have to look out for?

Below is a lists of features of patterns that a left handed crocheter, may need to reverse or recalibrate:

- Video tutorials

- Photo tutorials

- Charts / Stitch Diagrams

- Colour work or cables or other decorative patterns

HOW TO CROCHET LEFT-HANDED

- Patterns which refer to left side / right side

Using right haded crochet video and photo tutorials as a left handed crocheter

As the majority of people are right handed, a lot of crochet tutorials are created by and or for right hand crocheters.

If you're working these as a left hander then your work will be a mirror image of what is seen on screen or paper. So you will need to flip either the image or your work (mentally or by using a mirror) to compare the two.

By now this comes naturally to me, but if you're new to crochet then it can really throw you off.

If you can, especially if you're newer to crochet I recommend seeking out left handed resources.

Because I am left handed I can only create my tutorial left handed. But I use my video editing software to simply mirror the video so it becomes suitable for right handers.

Most video editing software will now allow you to flip the video, making it relatively simple to turn a right handed tutorial into a left handed one. For creators and designers, there are now very few barriers for people to provide videos for both left and right handed crocheters.

Handedness is an important feature to include for those who wish to

HOW TO CROCHET LEFT-HANDED

be inclusive. It takes a little extra time, and disk space to create a copy, but it's not like reinventing the wheel.

Similarly, photos taken of a right handed crochet stitch for example can be mirrored to make them left handed and vice versa.

The image below is reversed / flipped so this echos what a right handed crocheter would see. I imagine, depending on whether you are left or right handed, one of these two pictures looks rather odd to you.

HOW TO CROCHET LEFT-HANDED

You can tell the first image is left handed as the hook is working along the row from left to right. Whereas on the second image, the hook is working from right to left (so is a right handed image).

Whilst I could create photo tutorials using both pictures – essentially creating a duplicate tutorial – the reality is that this is not very practical. What I do instead is to add a note at the start of a tutorial stating whether the images are left or right handed.

It actually took me a while to realise these tutorial photos might be confusing to a right hander, so some of my older tutorials may still

HOW TO CROCHET LEFT-HANDED

require that additional note.

Left handed crochet charts

Crochet charts are something where handedness needs to be considered. However, these can be easier to mitigate than mirroring.

Below is the chart used for the circle colourwork in my chakra shawl pattern.

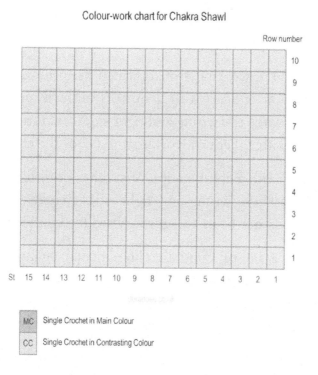

Colour-work chart for Chakra Shawl

MC Single Crochet in Main Colour

CC Single Crochet in Contrasting Colour

For a typical right haded crochet chart, one would start at the bottom right and follow the chart up the rows back and forth to create the image.

If I were to follow this chart (as a left hander) bottom up from right to left, I would end up with a mirror image of it.

In this example, the shape is symmetrical so it would make no difference. But for an asymmetric chart, this could be problematic.

To correct the mirror image issue as a left hander you could follow the chart from left to right instead (still working from bottom to top as the row direction doesn't change).

Alternatively, if you're working a chart which uses the same stitches throughout, and you end up with a mirror image by mistake, you should be able to switch the wrong and right sides (i.e. turn your fabric over) and end up with a piece of work that matches the chart.

If you are working with a combination of stitches or different stitches on different rows where wrong and right sides matter (are not just nominal), then it will not be as straight forward to flip the fabric over.

It can take quite a bit of mind bending mental agility to reverse diagrams in your head and factor in wrong / right sides. So for more complex charts, I recommend left handers swatch a small section to check that it's going to come out the right way around.

Directionality of charts can be important when working with text patterns for example, where it really matters which way the pattern works up.

HOW TO CROCHET LEFT-HANDED

Left handed crochet stitch diagrams

Generally speaking, most left handers can follow right handed charts just fine.

The chart below is a typical example of a crochet pattern worked in rows. It is followed from the bottom up.

Basic Filet Crochet Chart

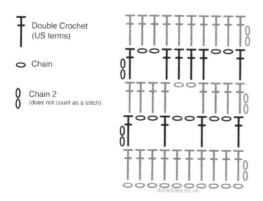

Double Crochet
(US terms)

Chain

Chain 2
(does not count as a stitch)

When working with filet crochet charts, an empty 'space' is one double crochet (US terms) two chains and skip two stitches - this will look different for right and left handers:

Right
Hand
Space

Left
Hand
Space

Here the starting chain is made and the first row is worked from right to left, starting in the 3rd chain from the hook. Double crochets are

32

worked along the row to the end and the work is turned ready for the second row.

The second row in the diagram is shown worked left to right. In practice however, because you turn your work at the end of the row, a right handed crocheter would still be working from right to left.

So essentially everyone is doing a bit of flipping when it comes to these kind of stitch diagrams.

As long as you keep your rows relative, there shouldn't be an issue with left and right handers using a simple chart like this one.

The same issues apply with wrong / right sides as discussed previously with grid based charts.

Below the chart, I have added a little caveat which is specific to fillet crochet (which I will talk about in another post soon) but to create a 'hole,' which is characteristic of fillet crochet, you work 1 double crochet, chain 2 and miss 2 stitches.

I have shown what each of these stitches would look like for left and right handers as you actually work, in order to highlight the differences. Once again, they are simply mirror images of one another.

Circular charts can be a little more confusing to work with but, generally speaking, as a left hander, you should just be able to follow them clockwise instead of anti-clockwise.

You may find some of the starting chains or slip stitches for joining

HOW TO CROCHET LEFT-HANDED

are a little misleading in some cases, so do watch out for those.

Left handed accommodations for complex stitch patterns and crochet cables

There are some instances where, when following a written pattern, it is important to know in advance that your work will be a mirror image of the one pictured (if you use a different dominant hand to the maker of the sample).

This design has an interrupted cable pattern where the breaks are on an angle. In the picture below you can see that the break in the cabe slopes upwards (from bottom up) from left to right.

However, if you're a right hander working on this pattern your breaks will slope upwards from right to left.

When I first released the pattern, I had one right handed maker who was sure they were doing something wrong because the slope was the other way. As a consequence, they tried to fudge it to make it look like the picture and ended up in a bit of a pickle.

This pattern had been tested but the issue hadn't come up there. I have since updated the pattern so it's clear that there will be difference with left / right handers.

I'll show you a close up of the swatches, which make it more obvious why it's important to be aware of the implication of left / right handed makes, even if you don't need to change anything.

HOW TO CROCHET LEFT-HANDED

Below is the left handed swatch which matches the sweater. The image immedately after is the right handed / flipped version. You can see that if you were trying to make your fabric look like the wrong picture you would end up in a mess.

HOW TO CROCHET LEFT-HANDED

I actually think that it's right handed crocheters who are working from left handed samples who are more likely to fall prey to this issue. I'm generalising here, but I think right handers rarely have to think about handedness because they are in the majority, so it may not occur to them it could be a difference.

My advice here, regardless of handedness, is that if something doesn't seem right with how your project is working up, check in with the designer.

In the second picture above, there is a telltale sign that the image has been flipped. If you look closely at the hook, you can see that the text stating the hook size is reversed. One to check for if you think something is backwards.

How to work with patterns that refer to left and right sides as a left hander

Some patterns, particularly garments, will often refer to left and right sides. This might be for something like neck shaping or cardigan fronts or sleeve / shoulder shaping.

If you're a left hander working from a pattern written by a right hander then the general rule of thumb is to substitute right for left in the pattern and it will all come up roses.

As a left handed pattern designer however, I find this over complex and prone to cause confusion – especially as I am usually already reversing it once from left to right hand.

Instead I prefer to use the terms first and second side.

Instructions are generally relative so there is a natural first and second side. That or it doesn't matter which side you tackle first but the second needs to be different to the first.

One thing I've learned for writing patterns is always to make the instructions as simple as possible. I find that replacing references to left and right with relative terms helps with this simplicity.

How do I teach someone to crochet if they have a different dominant hand to me?

Hard truth to start with… this can be tricky!

When I was a kid, my mum used to get us knit dishcloths for my grandmother at Christmas. She (as a right hander) taught me the basic knit stitch but when I wanted to learn more, she just couldn't get her head around it so my knitting career stalled aged 7…

Before the wonder of youtube, these things were much harder!

When I was learning to crochet, finding good left handed tutorials on youtube was like discovering a goldmine for me. They are thankfully much more common now than they were ten years ago.

Youtube is great for left handers, but wha about teaching in person?

The best tip I have seen for teaching opposite handed people face to face is literally to do just that. Sit opposite and just have them mirror everything you do. Try not to mention left and right though as that can muddy the waters.

Although I don't tend to tech in person, I tried this with my nephew one holiday a couple of years ago and he picked it up pretty quickly.

How can right handed crochet designers help left handed

HOW TO CROCHET LEFT-HANDED

crocheters?

I want to end with a bit of a summary of the issues which impact left handed crocheters and to consider how we can be more accommodating of those who work differently to us.

This section is also designed to help those of you who write crochet patterns or make crochet tutorials to better serve your left handed makers.

If a pattern is thoughtfully written then there is no reason that any significant changes need to be made for left handed crocheters. However, here is a quick checklist of points to consider in any crochet pattern or tutorial.

1. Clarify whether images or videos are right or left handed. Link to alternatives if they are available.

2. If you include directional instructions for charts / diagrams, make sure there is also an instruction appropriate for left handers. Don't just assuming lefties will know to change it.

3. If the pattern is likely to look significantly different if mirror imaged, make sure that left handers will know to expect a reversal.

4. Where possible, a pattern or tutorial should refrain from using left and right descriptors and use relative terms such as first and second or before and after / previous and next instead.

This may refer to left side or right sides, but is also relevant to

HOW TO CROCHET LEFT-HANDED

instructions such as 'insert hook in stitch to the left.' Try something like, 'insert hook in previous stitch' instead.

5. If you have your patterns or tutorials tested, try to make sure you include a left handed tester and ask them to look out for any differences from the right handed sample.

I hope that, wether left or right handed, or ambidextrous, you have found this a useful breakdown of how crochet is different for those with different dominant hands.

If you've come across any issues that I haven't mentioned here, I would love to hear them, so please do share your experience in the comments.

LEARN TO CROCHET LEFT HANDED

CROCHET STITCHES

All crochet stitches are based on the action of a loop pulled through another loop with a hook.

When crocheting, left handed people work from left to right.

When learning the basic steps, begin with 8ply yarn and a 3.50mm hook OR 4ply yarn and a 2.50mm hook, so that each stitch is clearly visible.

Practise the simple steps first before attempting the finer threads.

In all crocheting, pick up the two top threads of each stitch unless otherwise stated.

The two top threads consist of a front and a back loop.

HOW TO BEGIN TO CROCHET

HOW TO CROCHET LEFT-HANDED

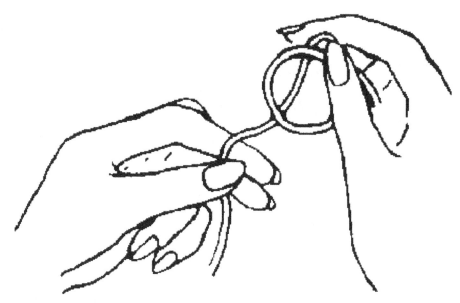

STEP 1.

TO MAKE A LOOP

1. Grasp the thread near the end between the thumb and the forefinger of the right hand.

2. With the left hand, make a loop by lapping the long thread over the short thread.

3. Hold this loop in place between the thumb and the forefinger of the right hand.

HOW TO CROCHET LEFT-HANDED

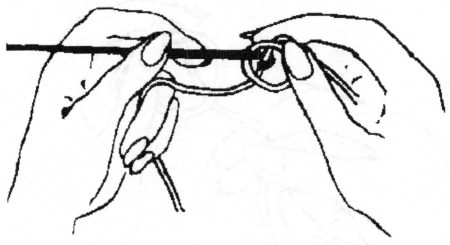

STEP 2.

1. With the left hand, take hold of the broad bar of the hook as you would a pencil.

2. Insert the hook through the loop and under the long thread. With the left hand, catch the long end of the thread. Draw the loop through.

3. Do not remove the hook from the thread.

HOW TO CROCHET LEFT-HANDED

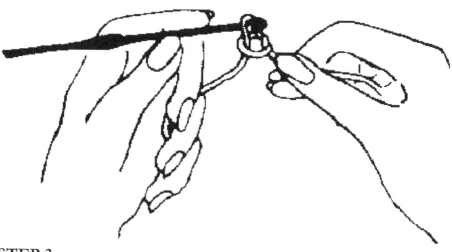

STEP 3.

1. Pull the short end and the ball thread in opposite directions to bring the loop around the end of the hook, but not too tight.

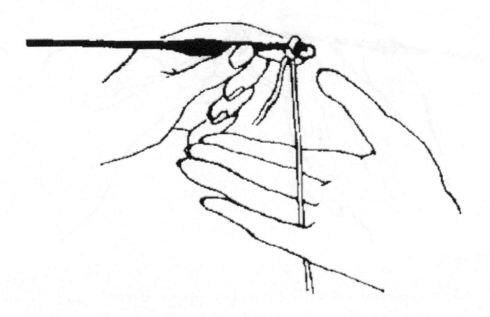

STEP 4.

WHAT TO DO WITH THE RIGHT HAND

1. Measure with your eye about 10cm along the ball thread from the loop on the hook.

2. At about this point, insert the thread between the ring finger and the little finger, having the palm of the hand facing up.

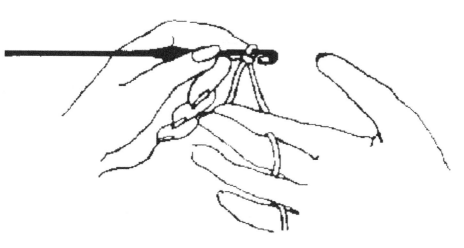

STEP 5.

1. Bring the thread towards the back, under the little finger and the ring finger, over the middle finger and under the forefinger towards the thumb.

HOW TO CROCHET LEFT-HANDED

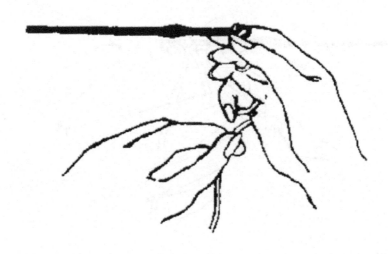

STEP 6.

1. Grasp the hook and the loop between the thumb and the forefinger of the right hand.

2. Gently pull the ball thread so that it lies around the fingers firmly, but not tightly.

3. Catch the knot of the loop between the thumb and the forefinger.

HOW TO CROCHET LEFT-HANDED

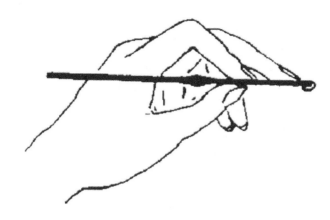

STEP 7.

WHAT TO DO WITH THE LEFT HAND

1. Take hold of the broad bar of the hook as you would a pencil.

2. Bring the middle finger forward to rest near the tip of the hook.

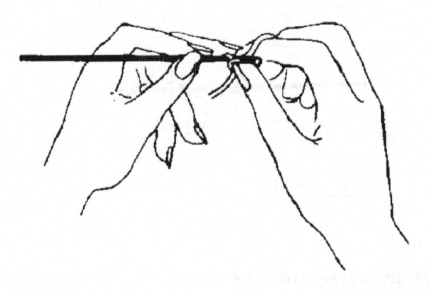

STEP 8.

1. Adjust the fingers of the right hand, the middle finger is bent to regulate the tension, the ring and the little fingers control the thread. The motion of the hook in the left hand and the thread in the right hand should be free and even. Ease comes with practice.

CHAIN (ch) is the basis of all crocheting. Chain is used to begin crocheting, to obtain height at the beginning of a row, and in patterns where an opening or a hole is required. When crocheting the starting row (foundation chain), work the chain stitches more loosely than the following rows.

HOW TO CROCHET LEFT-HANDED

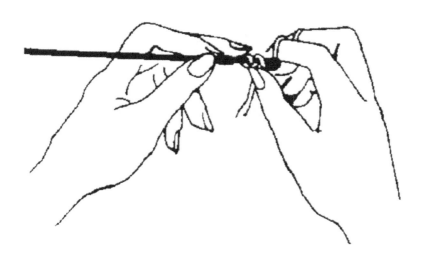

STEP 9.

CHAIN (ch)

1. Pass the hook under the thread and catch the thread with the hook. This is called **"thread over"** or yarn over hook.

2. Draw the thread through the loop on the hook. This makes one **chain (ch).** The loop on the hook is not counted as a stitch.

HOW TO CROCHET LEFT-HANDED

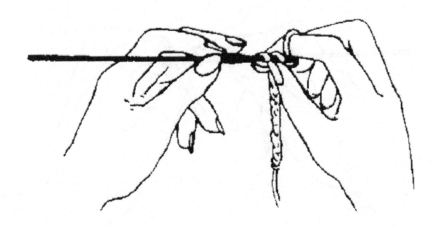

STEP 10.

1. Repeat Step 9 until you have as many chain (ch) as you need – one loop always remains on the hook.

2. Always keep the thumb and the forefinger of the right hand near the stitch on which you are working.

3. Practise making chain stitches until they are even in size.

SLIP STITCH (sl st)

HOW TO CROCHET LEFT-HANDED

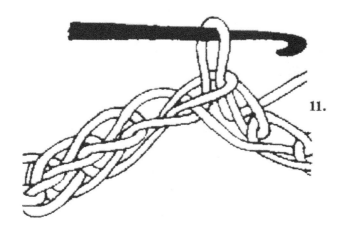

Slip stitching is used to move across the row without creating depth and to join rounds in circular crocheting.

Insert the hook from the front, under the two top threads of the stitch next to the hook, thread over and draw it through the stitch AND the loop on the hook in one movement.

DOUBLE CROCHET (dc)

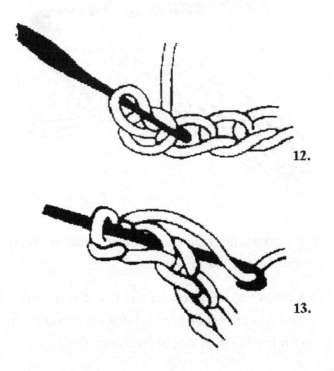

12.

13.

Make a length of chain, insert the hook from the front, under the two top threads of the 2nd chain from the hook. (Fig 12)

Thread over. (Fig 13)

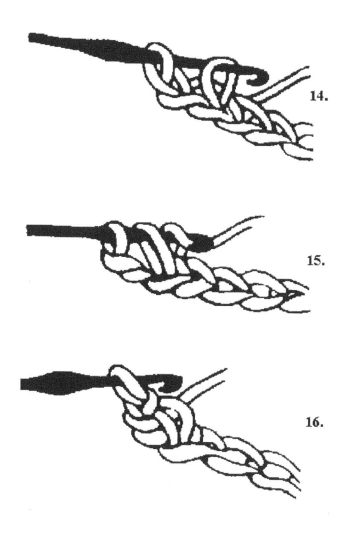

Draw it through the chain, there are now two loops on the hook. (Fig 14)

Thread over. (Fig 15)

Draw through the two loops, one loop will remain on the hook. One double crochet (dc) now completed. (Fig 16)

For next dc, insert the hook under the two top threads of the next stitch and repeat as before.

HALF TREBLE (htr)

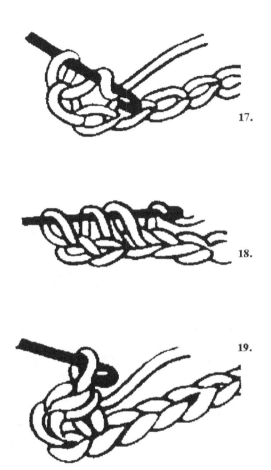

17.

18.

19.

Make a length of chain, thread over, insert the hook from the front, under the two top threads of the 3rd ch from the hook (Fig 17).

Thread over, and draw it through this ch. There are now three loops on the hook, thread over (Fig 18), and draw it through all three loops, one loop will remain on the hook.

One half treble (1htr) completed (Fig 19).

For the next htr, thread over, insert the hook under the two top threads of the next ch and repeat as before.

TREBLE (tr)

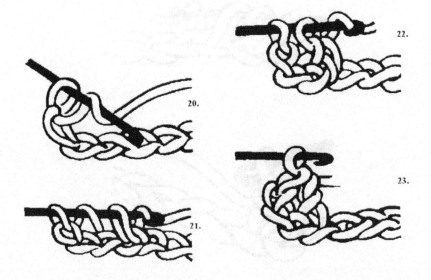

Make a length of chain, thread over, insert the hook from the front, under the two top threads of the 4th ch from the hook (Fig 20).

Thread over, and draw it through this ch. There are now 3 loops on the hook, thread over (Fig 21).

Now draw it through 2 loops, 2 loops will remain on the hook, thread over (Fig 22).

Now draw it through the remaining 2 loops, 1 loop will remain on the hook. One treble (1tr) completed (Fig 23).

For the next tr, thread over, insert the hook under the two top threads of the next ch and repeat as before.

DOUBLE TREBLE (dtr)

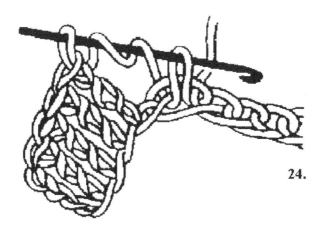

24.

HOW TO CROCHET LEFT-HANDED

Make a length of chain, thread over twice, insert the hook from the front, under the two top threads of the 5th ch from the hook, thread over, and draw it through the ch. There are now 4 loops on the hook, thread over, and draw it through 2 loops, 3 loops will remain on the hook, thread over again, and draw it through 2 loops, 2 loops will remain on the hook, thread over again, and draw it through the remaining 2 loops, 1 loop will remain on the hook. One double treble (1dtr) now completed.

For next dtr, thread over twice, insert the hook under the two top threads of the next ch and repeat as before (Fig 24).

TRIPLE TREBLE (triptr)

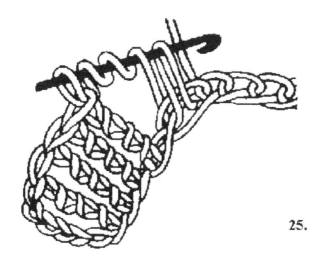

25.

Make a length of chain, thread over three times, insert the hook from the front, under the two top threads of the 6th ch from the hook, thread over, and draw it through the ch. There are now 5 loops on the hook, thread over, and draw it through 2 loops, 4 loops will remain on the hook, thread over again, and draw it through 2 loops, 3 loops will remain on the hook, thread over again, and draw it through 2 loops, 2 loops will remain on the hook, thread over again, and draw it through the remaining 2 loops, 1 loop will remain on the hook. One triple treble (triptr) now completed.

For next triptr, thread over three times, insert the hook under the two top threads of the next ch and repeat as before (Fig 25).

QUADRUPLE TREBLE (quadtr)

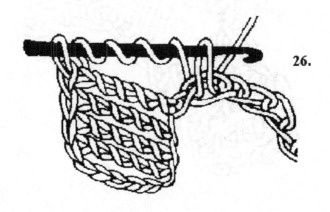

26.

Make a length of chain, thread over four times, insert the hook from the front, under the two top threads of the 7th ch from the hook, thread over, and draw it through the ch. There are now 6 loops on the hook, thread over, and draw it through 2 loops, 5 loops will remain on the hook, thread over again, and draw it through 2 loops, 4 loops will remain on the hook, thread over again, and draw it through 2 loops, 3 loops will remain on the hook, thread over again, and draw it through 2 loops, 2 loops will remain on the hook, thread over again, and draw it through the remaining 2 loops, 1 loop will remain on the hook. One quadruple treble (1quadtr) now completed.

HOW TO CROCHET LEFT-HANDED

For the next quadtr, thread over four times, insert the hook under the two top threads of the next ch and repeat as before (Fig 26).

Back to INDEX

QUINTUPLE TREBLE (quintr)

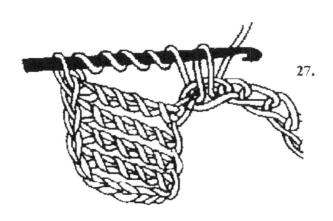

27.

Make a length of chain, thread over five times, insert the hook from the front, under the two top threads of the 8th ch from the hook, thread over, and draw it through the ch. There are now 7 loops on the hook, thread over, and draw it through 2 loops, 6 loops will remain on the hook, thread over again, and draw it through 2 loops, 5 loops will remain on the hook, thread over again, and draw it through 2 loops, 4 loops will remain on the hook, thread over again, and draw it through 2 loops, 3 loops will remain on the hook, thread over again, and draw it through 2 loops, 2 loops will remain on the hook, thread over again, and draw it through the remaining 2 loops, 1 loop will remain on the hook. One quintuple treble (1quintr) now completed.

For next quintuple tr, thread over five times, insert the hook under the 2 top threads of the next ch and repeat as before (Fig 27).

READING PATTERNS

If the pattern is written in rows, crochet the first row then turn the work, continue the next row to the end, turn the work again and then proceed with the 3rd and following rows, turning at the end of each row.

If the pattern is written in rounds, crochet the first round, ending with a slip stitch into the top of the beginning stitch of the round. DO NOT TURN the work between rounds.

When the instructions are inside a bracket, repeat them as many times as specified, for example (5ch, 1dc in next dc) 6 times, this means to work all in the brackets 6 times only.

An * (asterisk) in a pattern means that the instruction after the * is repeated as many times as specified, in addition to the original instruction that followed the asterisk. For example, (Miss 2tr, * 1tr in next tr, 5ch; repeat from * to last 1tr, 1tr in last tr), means to miss the first 2tr, then work 1tr in the next tr and make 5ch, then continue to repeat doing 1tr in the next tr and 5ch until 1tr remains, then work 1tr in the last tr.

INCREASING

Precise instructions for increasing are usually given in each pattern. However, a simple increase will consist of working two stitches (instead of one), into one stitch of the previous row. This may be done at either end of the row or in any part of the row. The pattern will usually specify the correct procedure.

DECREASING

When decreasing, the pattern will specify the method to be used.

"Miss one stitch" – miss the next stitch and work into the following stitch. This will decrease the number of stitches by one. Also referred to as "skip 1" in some patterns.

"Work 2sts tog" – (work 2 stitches together) This is achieved by not finishing either of the next 2 stitches, but leaving the last loop of each stitch on the hook in addition to the loop already on the hook. Thread over, and pull the yarn through all the loops to form 1 loop on the hook. This produces a less obvious space.

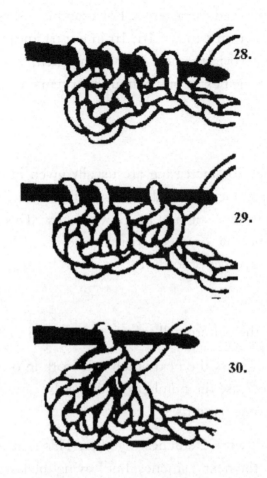

For example to "work 2sts tog" or decrease over treble, complete the first treble to the point where there are 2 loops on the hook. Work the next treble until there are 4 loops on the hook (Fig 28).

Thread over and draw the thread through 2 loops (Fig 29), thread over again and draw the thread through the remaining 3 loops. One loop remains on the hook. This is often referred to as treble decrease or decrease treble. (Fig 30)

When decreasing at the beginning of a row, simply slip stitch over the required number of stitches to be decreased, then work the turning chain and continue the row.

When decreasing at the end of a row, work to within the number of stitches to be decreased, turn work and continue the next row.

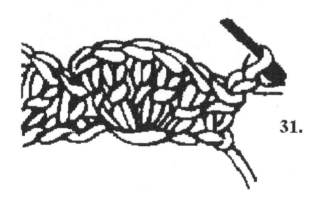

31.

Increases and decreases in stitches and changing the type of stitch are the basis of all patterns. For example, 1dc in next st, miss 2sts, 5tr in next st, miss 2sts, 1dc in next st (Fig 31), forms a shell design.

CROCHETING IN ROWS

Make a length of chain (foundation chain). Depending on the stitch to be used, extra chain will need to be added to form the height of the stitch. These chain count as the first stitch unless otherwise stated. Some patterns say to "miss" a certain number of stitches at the beginning of the first row. This also gives the required height. Use the table below as a guide.

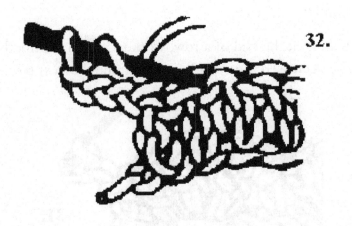

32.

When crocheting in rows, for example in trebles, work a foundation row and when the last treble is completed, turn the work so that the reverse side is facing. Work 3 chain (turning chain) for height, and because the turning chain will count as the first stitch of this new row, miss the last worked stitch of the previous row and work the next treble into the top of the next treble (Fig 32).

Remember to always insert the hook under the two top threads of each stitch, unless the pattern states otherwise.

Continue across the row. The last treble of the row will be worked into the top of the turning chain, that is, into the 3rd chain of the beginning 3ch of the last row.

Some patterns, in which the turning chain does not count as the first stitch at the beginning of the row, require you to work into the last stitch of the previous row, and in this case you do not work a stitch into the turning chain at the end of the row.

The turning chain table is used as a guide only when determining the number of stitches required for a turning chain. Depending on the type and texture of thread / yarn used, the number of chain can be varied. Similarly, rows of dc, htr, dtr, and other sts are worked, varying the height of the turning chain.

Stitch used in row	Turning chain
double crochet	1ch
half treble	2ch
treble	3ch
double treble	4ch
triple treble	5ch
quadruple treble	6ch
quintuple treble	7ch

BREAK OFF

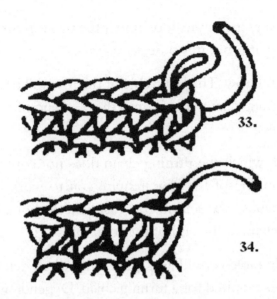

33.

34.

BREAK OFF is to finish off or end off. Simply cut the thread about 8 – 10cm long. Bring the cut end through the last remaining loop on the hook and pull tightly (Figs 33 and 34). Weave this end back into the main part of the work with a blunt needle.

TO CROCHET IN ROUNDS

HOW TO CROCHET LEFT-HANDED

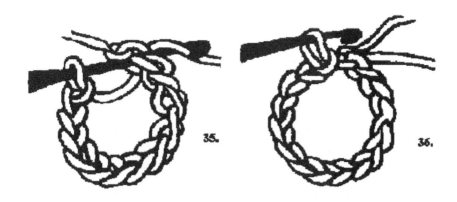

When crocheting in rounds, unless stated in the pattern, never turn the work between the rounds. Each stitch is still worked under the two top threads of the stitch in the previous round. A "right side" will be noticeable in the crocheted piece. Rounds are joined with a slip stitch (sl st) [Figs 35 and 36]. Rounds can be worked in a variety of stitches. The example below is worked in treble only.

To begin, make 4ch. Join with a sl st into the first ch to form a ring. Do not twist the work.

Round 1. 3ch, (this is for height and will count as one st). Work 11 treble into the centre of the ring. Join the round with a sl st into the 3rd ch of the beginning 3ch. (12tr)

Round 2. 3ch, 1tr in same place as sl st, 2tr in each of the other tr, join the round with a sl st into the 3rd ch of the beginning 3ch. (24tr) This is increasing in every stitch.

In the next round the stitches must be increased evenly, so proceed as follows:

Round 3. 3ch, * 2tr in next tr, 1tr in the next tr; repeat from * to last st, 2tr in this st. Join the round with a sl st into the 3rd ch of the beginning 3ch. (36tr) The increase was made in every second stitch.

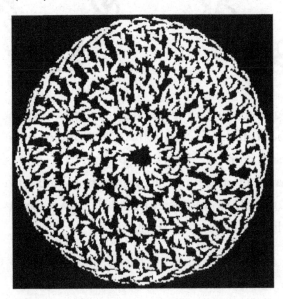

Increasing is achieved by working a required number of stitches into one stitch. Most patterns state when to increase and the method to use. The aim is to increase at a rate that allows the crocheting to remain flat.

Variations of terminology:

"Round 1" may read "1st round", and "into the 3rd ch of the beginning 3ch" may read "into the top of the turning ch".

CLUSTERS AND POPCORNS are commonly used in edges, motifs and patterns. Any number of stitches can be used and so can any combinations of any type of stitch. It is common for most patterns to use the one stitch for height.

CLUSTER (cl)

A cluster may vary from two to six stitches. It may be worked over a given number of stitches, into one stitch or into a space. Following are examples of these variations.

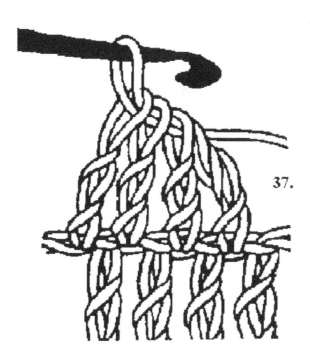

37.

HOW TO CROCHET LEFT-HANDED

1. A 4dtr cluster over 4 stitches. Leaving the last loop of each stitch on the hook, work 1dtr into each of the following 4 stitches, thread over hook and draw it through all the remaining 5 loops on the hook (Fig 37).

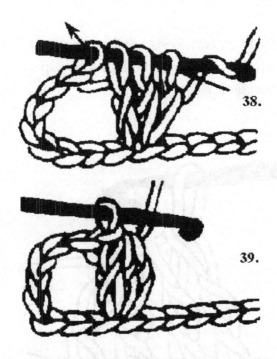

38.

39.

2. A 3tr cluster worked into one stitch. Leaving the last loop of each stitch on the hook, work 3tr into the one stitch, thread over hook, pull through all 4 loops on the hook (Figs 38 and 39).

40.

3. A 3dtr cluster worked into a space or loop. Leaving the last loop of each stitch on the hook, work 3dtr into the space of the previous row, thread over hook and draw it through all the remaining 4 loops on the hook (Fig 40).

POPCORN

A popcorn is a group of three or more stitches worked into the same stitch of the previous row and is completed as follows:

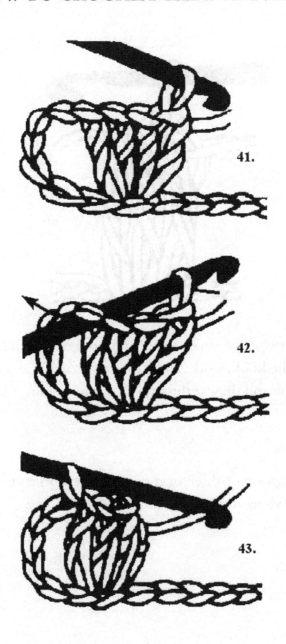

41.

42.

43.

HOW TO CROCHET LEFT-HANDED

To make a 4tr popcorn. Work 4tr into the same stitch (Fig 41).

Remove the loop from the hook, insert the hook into the top of the first treble of this group, then into the loop just dropped (Fig 42).

Pull the loop through the first treble (Fig 43). A popcorn is usually, but not always, followed by 1 or more chain to define the popcorn.

HOW TO LEARN LEFT-HANDED CROCHET

Left-handed crochet is as common as the number of people who are naturally left-handed. In spite of this, most crochet instructions are written for right-handed crafters. As a leftie, it can feel like the craft world has left you out. Luckily, that's changing, thanks to a number of motivated designers who have created tutorials and patterns for left-handed crafters. Even without those resources, though, it doesn't have to be difficult to learn how to crochet left-handed. The following resources and tips will get you started.

HOW TO CROCHET LEFT-HANDED

There's No "Right" Way to Learn

The first thing you need to know is that everyone crochets a little differently. So, there is no one "correct" way of doing it; there are many possible variations of correct when it comes to crochet. This is true whether or not you are left-handed.

One of the things that people do differently when learning how to crochet is that they hold their crochet hook a certain way. People often use either a "knife grip" or a "pencil grip" but may have their own variations of either one. Left-handed crocheters are no more likely to use one type of grip over the other in comparison with right-handed crocheters.

Right vs. Left: What's the Difference?

The only real difference between left-handed and right-handed crochet is what hand you hold the hook in and which direction you work a row. In right-handed crochet, the hook is held in the right hand. With a few exceptions for specific niches of crochet, the right-handed crafter works stitches from the right to the left. In left-handed crochet, it's the exact opposite: hold the hook in the left hand and work the stitches from left to right.

How to Learn

There are a few common ways that people go about learning left-handed crochet:

- **Follow left-handed crochet tutorials:** These are readily available online and include both written tutorials with photos and video tutorials. Many people prefer video tutorials when first learning crochet.

- **Have a left-handed crafter teach you**: Ask at your local craft store if there is a crochet teacher who is available to teach a left-handed crafter.

- **Sit opposite a right-handed crochet teacher**: This will allow you to follow what they are doing while working as the mirror image using your left hand.

- **Learn to crochet right-handed**: This used to be the only option. It's not a top choice for most people, but it's an option. If you're ambidextrous or find that you can easily crochet right-handed even though you're a lefty then it's always an option to just learn "regular" crochet.

It is worth noting that you will be using both hands in crochet regardless of which hand holds the hook. The dominant hand typically holds the hook, but the non-dominant hand stays busy working the yarn and holding the work-in-progress.

Reverse Images in Graphic Crochet

When working with written crochet patterns, you don't need to do anything differently as a left-handed crocheter. However, when you are working from crochet graphs and charts, you will want to reverse the image before beginning crochet. If you don't, then your left-handed crochet work will have an image that is the opposite of intended. That can be okay with symmetrical images but doesn't work for words and asymmetrical images.

Teaching Left-Handed Crochet

As a teacher, you can adapt your own crochet style to other-handed crafters. As mentioned before, one option is to sit across from the crafter so that they can mirror your style. You may also wish to create crochet video tutorials, and you can use video editing software to actually horizontally flip the image in order to create a left-handed crochet tutorial from your right-handed crochet video.

3 TIPS FOR TEACHING LEFT-HANDED CROCHET

Out of my 6 children, 5 of them are girls. So, naturally I want them all to love crochet as much as me. I taught the oldest 2 girls when they were 7 & 6 years old. At the time my 4th child (3rd daughter) was 5 year old. She wanted to learn also, but because she's left-handed, had some learning struggles, and was only 5, she had a very hard time. We put it down for a couple years and tried to pick it up again, but she still wasn't getting it.

I finally did some research and came up with 3 different methods that left-handers have used to learn to crochet. We.tried.them.**all**....

- **The mirror effect** – Have them sit facing you. The concept is to have them do exactly what they see you doing as if looking in a mirror. This will help them be able to visualize without having to reverse everything in their mind. The mirror effect will do that part for them.

- **Teach *yourself* to crochet left-handed** – Teach yourself to crochet left-handed so you can have a better understanding of how to teach it. Yes, *it's a stretch*, but I actually tried this to help my daughter. It gave me a new found respect for trying something challenging. It was like learning to crochet all over again! While it did help my daughter a bit, it wasn't the method she ended up going with.

81

HOW TO CROCHET LEFT-HANDED

- **Have them try to crochet right-handed** – Have them try to crochet right-handed. While this doesn't seem like the most logical way, some people find it easier than actually using their left hand. I have 2 daughters that do everything with their primary hand but have one (maybe two) tasks that are easier with the opposite hand. Honestly this was the last technique I tried with my daughter, but it is ultimately what worked best for her.

Because everyone learns differently, you will need to try them to see which will work for you, or whomever you're teaching. Left-handed crochet can be just as fun and rewarding as doing it right-handed. Whether you are teaching a child, or an adult, just keep trying and see what works best.

HOW TO CROCHET LEFT HANDED TREBLE CROCHET STITCH

For all the wonderful odd-balls out there who are left-handed this tutorial is just for you. Learn step-by-step how to make a treble crochet stitch left-handed. The images will really help you out and all we want you to do is to learn! There aren't many left-handed tutorials out there and we understand how difficult it is to not be able to learn comfortably. Please try this out if you're a beginner.

1. To begin a row of treble crochet, chain 3.

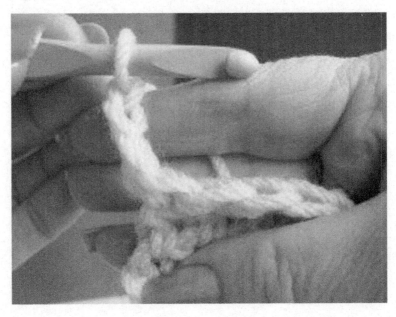

2. Yarn over the hook 2 times.

3. Insert the hook through the next stitch.

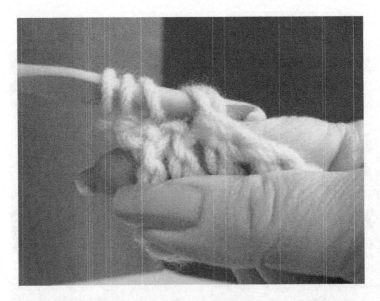

1. Yarn over the hook.

2. Pull the yarn through the first loop.

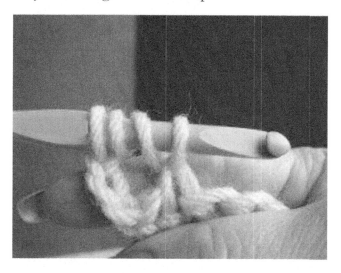

3. Yarn over the hook, and pull through the first 2 loops.

4. Yarn over the hook, and pull through two more loops.

5. Yarn over the hook, and pull through the remaining 2 loops.

HOW TO CROCHET LEFT-HANDED

One treble crochet stitch formed. Repeat steps 2 to

6. Photo shows one row of treble crochet stitches completed.

HOW TO CROCHET A POPCORN STITCH LEFT-HANDED

This How to Crochet a Popcorn Stitch left-handed video tutorial makes mastering this specific crochet stitch a breeze. This stitch is a series of five stitches all worked into one stitch causing a kind of bobble affect. This specific crochet pattern is fantastic for baby blankets and other project types that really thrive on that kind of different unique texture. Plus, this crochet video takes a stitch that looks complicated and makes it a breeze to understand how to complete it. It is best to start with a smaller swatch for this stitch and work your way up to bigger projects!

Difficulty Level Easy

HOW TO CROCHET LEFT-HANDED

Materials List

- Yarn

- Crochet Hook

How to Crochet the Popcorn Stitch

Instructions to Crochet the Popcorn Stitch

1. Yarn over and insert your hook into the stitch. Yarn over and pull up a loop.

2. Yarn over pull through the first two loops, yarn over and pull through the final two stitches. This will complete your first double crochet.

3. Repeat this four more times so you have five stitches.

4. Pull your hook out of your single loop, but be sure to not pull too hard or lose the loop.

5. Insert your hook into the first stitch from your five stitches, farthest away from your loop, and insert your hook into that stitch, push your hook back through your loop and pull your loop through the stitch.

6. Chain one stitch.

7. Repeat this until you complete your project!

ONE SKEIN MINI CROCHET BLANKET PATTERN

Difficulty Level Easy

Crochet HookM/13 or 9 mm hook

Yarn Weight(4) Medium Weight/Worsted Weight and Aran (16-20 stitches to 4 inches)

Crochet Gauge3 sts x 1 row in dc = 1"

Finished Size20 x 40"

HOW TO CROCHET LEFT-HANDED

Materials List

- Yarn: Red Heart with Love, medium weight # 4, 1 skein Mint
- Hook: 9.0mm

Blanket

1. Ch 71.

2. **Row 1:** sc in second chain from hook and in each across (70 sts).

3. **Row 2:** Ch 3 (first dc), turn, * (dc, ch 1, dc) in next st, sk 1 st, repeat from * to last st, dc in last st.

4. **Row 3**: Ch 3, turn, puff stitch in each ch 1 space, dc in last st.

5. **Row 4:** Ch 3, turn, (dc, ch 1, dc) in top of each puff stitch, dc in last st.

6. **Rows 5-6:** Repeat Rows 3-4.

7. **Row 7-21**: Ch 3, turn; (dc, ch 1, dc) in each ch 1 space.

8. **Row 22**: Repeat Row 3.

9. **Row 23**: Repeat Row 4.

10. **Row 24**: Repeat Row 3.
11. **Rows 25:** Repeat Row 4.
12. **Row 26**: Ch 1, turn, sc in each st. Fasten off. Weave in ends.

Made in the USA
Las Vegas, NV
15 February 2024